GROWTH & STUDY GUIDE

The Remarkable Prayers *of the* Bible

Jim George

HARVEST HOUSE PUBLISHERS

EUGENE, OREGON

Cover by Terry Dugan Design, Minneapolis, Minnesota

Cover image © Nick Daly/Stone/Getty Images

THE REMARKABLE PRAYERS OF THE BIBLE GROWTH AND STUDY GUIDE
Copyright © 2006 Jim George
Published by Harvest House Publishers
Eugene, Oregon 97402
www.harvesthousepublishers.com

ISBN-13: 978-0-7369-1649-3
ISBN-10: 0-7369-1649-0

Printed in the United States of America

06 07 08 09 10 11 12 13 / BP-CF / 10 9 8 7 6 5 4 3 2 1

Contents

A Word for Your Journey into...

The Remarkable
Prayers of the Bible

Do you desire to make your prayer life richer? Then the Bible has the help you need. There you find not only God's instructions regarding prayer, but examples of His men and women who prayed. You can learn from these praying saints who, like you, loved God and desired to follow Him wholeheartedly.

In this study guide you will look at 12 of the great men and women in the Bible—Job, Hannah, Daniel, Mary, Paul, Jesus, and others. Through them and the scriptures in this exciting study, you will discover many priceless and practical lessons for your prayer life. You will

- peer deeply into the prayers prayed by God's people

- witness the character qualities that marked their lives

- see firsthand how prayer transformed their service to God

As a man or woman who loves God and longs to enjoy a special prayer relationship with Him, you will find this study to be a practical resource that offers biblical guidance. It will enrich, improve, and inspire your prayer life. In each lesson you will be asked to read the corresponding chapter from *The Remarkable Prayers of the Bible*

- look at the scriptures that describe the man or woman spotlighted

- examine the dominant godly character quality of the person being featured

- study through the prayers prayed by the remarkable persons in the Bible

- make note of immediate, useful personal applications for your prayer life

As you encounter and inspect the prayers of the Bible, you will find yourself being transformed, drawing closer to God, and serving Him more powerfully. You will discover remarkable prayer for yourself!

Chapter 1

$\mathcal{A}$braham...
a Man of Remarkable Faith

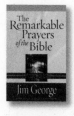

In *The Remarkable Prayers of the Bible,* read again each "Lesson to Learn about Prayer" from the chapter entitled "Abraham...a Man of Remarkable Faith." Which lesson about prayer offered you the greatest motivation or instruction for your prayer life, and why?

Which offered you the greatest challenge to your prayer life, and why?

The Testing of Faith

Write out a definition for *faith* from a dictionary.

What insights into the concept of *faith* do you gain after reading this definition?

How does the Bible define *faith*, according to Hebrews 11:1?

How important is faith, according to:

Hebrews 11:2—

Hebrews 11:6—

In addition to Abraham, what other Old Testament saints are named in Hebrews 11:4-34, known as God's "Hall of Faith"?

Read Romans 4:1-25. Abraham's life is used by Paul to contrast faith and the law. According to verses 1-8, on what basis did God consider Abraham righteous?

According to Genesis 15:1-6, what event verified Abraham's faith?

In Romans 4, Paul continues to use Abraham's encounters with God in the book of Genesis as an example of Abraham's growing faith. Briefly describe the scenes in these verses:

Genesis 17:15-22 —

Genesis 18:11-14 —

How does James 2:14-20 add to your understanding of true faith?

What event does James, in James 2:21-24, use to authenticate faith in the life of Abraham?

James also cited Rahab's faith in God in James 2:25-26. How does James sum up her trust in God?

According to Hebrews 10:35-36, what should the result of our faith be, even in the midst of difficulties and persecution?

Prayer in the Life of Abraham

Like most believers, Abraham's faith in God wavered, and at times he lapsed in prayer. But overall, Abraham was a person whose prayer life was intact and viable for significant periods of time. Therefore he provides for us a great model to follow.

Abraham answered God's call — Read Genesis 11:26–12:4.

What do you learn about Abraham from 11:26-32?

What was God's command to Abraham in Genesis 12:1?

What was God's promise to Abraham in 12:2-3?

How did Abraham's faith in God express itself in 12:4?

Abraham prayed to God and worshiped—Read Genesis 12:5-9.

What was Abraham's response to God's appearance and affir-
mation of the promise to give Abraham the land (verse 7)?

After traveling farther into the land, what was Abraham's two-
fold response (verse 8)?

What does this reveal about Abraham's growing trust in God?

Abraham sometimes forgot to pray—Read Genesis 12:10–
13:4.

In what ways did Abraham's fear and lack of trust in God's pro-
vision during the test of famine affect others?

How do you think your trust or lack of trust in God affects
those closest to you?

In what difficult areas is God calling you to have faith in Him, and how actively are you praying about those difficulties?

What do you learn about prayer or the lack of it from this episode from the life of Abraham?

Abraham responded in faith — Read Genesis 13.

What was Abraham and Lot's problem, and how did Abraham resolve it (verses 5-9)?

What did the way in which Abraham handled the problem reveal about his faith in God?

What clue does God give that indicates Lot's decision was not the best spiritual decision (verses 10-13)?

How did God honor Abraham's trust in Him (verses 14-17)?

How did God further encourage Abraham in Genesis 15:1-5, and what was Abraham's response in verse 6?

Abraham prayed for others — Read Genesis 18.

What promise did God make to Abraham in verse 10, and how did Sarah react to it (verse 12)?

What was Abraham's response to God's plan for dealing with the sinfulness of Sodom and Gomorrah (verses 22-32)?

From the dialogue between God and Abraham, what do you learn about:

God —

Abraham —

Intercessory prayer —

Abraham made a wrong decision — Read Genesis 16:1-16.

Briefly outline Sarah's idea for obtaining a child and Abraham's response (verses 1-2).

List some of the results of Abraham's wrong response (verses 3-6).

How do you, like Abraham and Sarah, tend to make unwise decisions when you become impatient with God's timing and try to rush things? Can you share an example?

From Abraham's wrong decision, what lessons do you learn about prayer and about waiting on the Lord?

Prayer Principles for Your Life

Write out the prayer principles from the life of Abraham below (see the principles on pages 22-24 in the book *The Remarkable Prayers of the Bible*):

1.

2.

3.

4.

5.

Which one or two principles encourage you most as you pray for the issues you are presently facing, and why?

What about Abraham's prayer life do you want to remember, and why?

Chapter 2

$\mathcal{M}$oses...
a Man of Remarkable Humility

 In *The Remarkable Prayers of the Bible*, read again each "Lesson to Learn about Prayer" from the chapter entitled "Moses...a Man of Remarkable Humility." Which lesson about prayer offered you the greatest motivation or instruction for your prayer life, and why?

Which offered you the greatest challenge to your prayer life, and why?

The Most Humble Man Alive

Man's humility—Besides Jesus Christ, Moses is the key example of humility in all of Scripture. What was God's evaluation of Moses in Numbers 12:3?

Humility is an attribute that appears consistently in the other biblical saints. How do these men describe themselves?

Abraham in Genesis 18:27—

David in 1 Chronicles 29:14—

Jeremiah in Jeremiah 1:6—

Paul in Acts 20:18-19—

How do these scriptures describe Jesus' humility?

Matthew 11:29—

Philippians 2:5-8—

Now read Philippians 2:3-5. What should our mindset be, as shown to us by Jesus?

What do these verses command us to do?

Ephesians 4:1-2—

Colossians 3:12—

1 Peter 5:5—

God's supremacy—How does the psalmist describe the majesty of God and His care for mankind in Psalm 113:1-9?

After this brief look at humility, how should God's supremacy, Jesus' actions and sacrifice, and the Bible's teaching regarding humility affect the way you view humility in your life?

Moses' life—Moses' life was divided into three phases.

Phase 1: From slave to prince (read Exodus 2:1-10)—

Describe Moses' early family life and how he came to live in Pharaoh's palace.

What details are added in Acts 7:19-23, and what about Moses' lifestyle might have contributed to his pride (verse 22)?

Phase 2: From prince to shepherd (read Exodus 2:11-15)—

What do you learn about Moses' compassion for his kinsmen? About his pride?

How did Moses' lifestyle change drastically in verse 15, and how might the 40 years as a lonely shepherd have changed Moses?

What did Stephen add in Acts 7:25 about Moses' prideful attitude as a prince and leader in Egypt?

Phase 3: From shepherd to leader—

How did Moses view himself, according to:

Exodus 3:11—

Exodus 4:10—

According to the following proverbs, what does God say about pride and humility?

Proverbs 15:33—

Proverbs 18:12—

Proverbs 22:4—

Proverbs 29:23—

Prayer in the Life of Moses

Moses was "very humble, more than all men who were on the face of the earth" (Numbers 12:3), but he was also "a righteous man" whose prayers brought about powerful results (James 5:16). Moses models the powerful habit of prayer, a habit that most assuredly contributed to his humility, and a habit you can develop and improve.

Moses prayed expecting a response — Read Exodus 3:1-10.

Where and how did God appear to Moses (verses 1-2)?

Briefly, what did God communicate to Moses in verses 3-10?

Now read Exodus 4:1-17. As God conversed with Moses and began to unfold His plan and purpose for Moses, what questions did Moses ask, and how did God answer in:

Exodus 3:11-12 —

Exodus 3:13-22 —

Exodus 4:1-9 —

Exodus 4:10-12 —

Exodus 4:13-17 —

At the end of this extended prayer conversation with God, what did Moses do in Exodus 4:18?

Moses prayed prayers of praise — Read Exodus 15:1-19.

List several of God's acts for which Moses gave praise.

Now read Deuteronomy 32:1-4, and quickly scan verses 5-43. List several of God's attributes for which Moses gave praise.

What elements of Moses' praises of God would you like to incorporate into your regular prayer times?

Moses prayed prayers of intercession—Read again (on pages 33-34 in your book) about Moses' prayers on behalf of others, and God's responses.

Who do you know who is in need of prayerful intercession? Note them here and on your prayer list, and be sure to pray for them.

Moses prayed to God instead of complaining to others—Read Exodus 15:22-25 and 17:1-6. How did Moses handle these times of crisis?

Moses, like all men and women, was not perfect. How did he mishandle the incident in Numbers 20:1-12?

Moses prayed for others regardless of how they treated him—Read (on pages 35-36 in your book) about Moses' prayers for others.

Who do you know who makes your life miserable, and how and when will you pray for them?

Moses prayed for sinners—Read Exodus 32:7-14 and 30-32.

To what extent did Moses care about the sinful behavior of the Israelites?

How does Moses' heart for his sinning brethren compare to Paul's heart for unbelieving Jews in Romans 9:3?

How does your heart for sinners compare to Moses' and Paul's hearts?

What changes need to be made in your heart's attitude?

Prayer Principles for Your Life

Write out the prayer principles from the life of Moses below (see pages 38-40 in your book):

1.

2.

3.

4.

5.

6.

Which one or two principles encourage you most as you pray for the issues you are presently facing, and why?

What about Moses' prayer life do you want to remember, and why?

Chapter 3

$\mathcal{H}$annah...
a Woman of Remarkable Gratitude

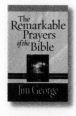

In *The Remarkable Prayers of the Bible*, read again each "Lesson to Learn about Prayer" from the chapter entitled "Hannah...a Woman of Remarkable Gratitude." Which lesson about prayer offered you the greatest motivation or instruction for your prayer life, and why?

Which offered you the greatest challenge to your prayer life, and why?

Gratitude Should Characterize a Christian's Life

In the Bible gratitude is described as showing thanks or expressing praise and thanksgiving. According to 1 Thessalonians 5:18, in what should we show gratitude to God?

What does Psalm 95:2 encourage us to do?

What do these verses teach us about expressing gratitude through prayer?

Psalm 50:14 —

Psalm 92:1-2 —

Philippians 4:6 —

Colossians 4:2 —

Hebrews 13:15 —

David—What did God promise David in 2 Samuel 7:15-16, and how did David respond in verse 18?

Daniel—In Daniel 2:16-18, what did Daniel do about Nebuchadnezzar's threats to kill all of the wise men?

How did God respond to Daniel (verse 19), and what was Daniel's response in verses 20-23 and Daniel 6:10?

Jonah—According to Jonah 2:9, what was Jonah's response to God after his deliverance from the great fish?

Simeon and Anna—How did these two righteous people respond upon seeing the Christ Child, according to Luke 2:28 and 38?

Paul—What was Paul's response in Acts 28:15 when fellow believers came to meet him on his way to Rome?

Mary—Read Luke 1:46-55, Mary's "Magnificat," and list a few expressions of her gratitude for God's covenant promises.

Jesus—Note how and for what Jesus expressed gratitude and thanksgiving in these passages:

Matthew 11:25—

Matthew 26:27—

John 6:11—

John 11:41—

Prayer in the Life of Hannah

In Hannah we witness a devout woman's actions and prayers when faced with multiple and extreme difficulties. We also catch a glimpse into her heart, a heart that instructs us in both praise and prayer, which should be part of our every breath.

Hannah prayed with the right attitude—Read 1 Samuel 1:1-8.

Describe Hannah's life situation:

Her heritage—

Her husband—

Her marriage—

Her tormentor—

Her agony—

Now read 1 Samuel 1:9-19. List the verses and details that evidence Hannah's attitude during prayer.

What is your present life situation, and how are you praying about it?

Do any attitude adjustments need to be made? Note them here and make plans to set about gaining the right attitude.

Hannah prayed in the right place — Read 1 Samuel 1:3-9.

Why was Hannah in Shiloh, and why was Shiloh important?

What are God's instructions to you about the right place to pray, according to Hebrews 4:16?

What instructions do these verses give about prayer and praying to God?

Mark 11:25 —

Luke 18:1 —

Ephesians 6:18 —

Philippians 4:6—

1 Thessalonians 5:17—

1 Peter 4:7—

Hannah prayed in the right way—Read 1 Samuel 1:10-16.

List the verses and details about the way in which Hannah prayed.

Which attitudes and methods exhibited by Hannah would you like to incorporate into your regular prayer times?

Read again (on pages 47-48 in your book) about the many different ways God's people have prayed. How do these ways and means of praying encourage you to call out to God in your distress, to pour out your soul before the Lord (as Hannah did—1 Samuel 1:15)?

According to Romans 8:26, why is it important for you to pray even when you are unsure of the right way to pray?

Hannah prayed for the right result—Read 1 Samuel 1:11-28.

How badly did Hannah desire a son (verse 11)?

In time, what did Hannah's desire and God's gracious answer require of Hannah (verses 22-28)?

According to James 4:1-3, why are some of our prayers not answered?

What should you pray for instead, according to 1 John 5:14?

Hannah prayed with the right response—Read 1 Samuel 2:1-11.

When the day finally arrived for Hannah to fulfill her vow to God and take her boy Samuel to live in the temple at Shiloh, what did Hannah do (verse 1)?

Review Hannah's prayer (verses 1-10) and the list on page 52 of your book that spotlights Hannah's worship and gratitude for God's power to keep His promises. What do you learn about:

Hannah's heart—

Hannah's understanding of God—

The nature of God—

God's sovereign control—

Ways to enhance your prayers—

Prayer Principles for Your Life

Write out the prayer principles from the life of Hannah below (see pages 55-57 in your book):

1.

2.

3.

4.

5.

Which one or two principles encourage you most as you pray for the issues you are presently facing, and why?

What about Hannah's prayer life do you want to remember, and why?

$\int$amuel...
a Man of Remarkable Faithfulness

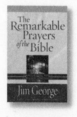

In *The Remarkable Prayers of the Bible*, read again each "Lesson to Learn about Prayer" from the chapter entitled "Samuel...a Man of Remarkable Faithfulness." Which lesson about prayer offered you the greatest motivation or instruction for your prayer life, and why?

Which offered you the greatest challenge to your prayer life, and why?

What Does It Take to Be Great?

Samuel was a great man because he was faithful to God in prayer and in obedience. Faithfulness is consistent with the nature of God, and should be evident in God's people.

What do these verses say about God?

Lamentations 3:23 —

1 Corinthians 1:9 —

1 Thessalonians 5:24 —

What do the following passages say about God's faithfulness?

Isaiah 25:1 —

Hebrews 10:23 —

Deuteronomy 7:9 —

2 Thessalonians 3:3 —

How should we respond to God's faithfulness?

Psalm 89:5 —

Psalm 92:1-2 —

Besides Samuel, others in the Bible modeled faithfulness. Read these verses and identify these faithful saints.

Numbers 12:7 —   Daniel 6:4 —

1 Samuel 12:14 —   1 Corinthians 4:17 —

Nehemiah 9:7-8 —   Ephesians 6:21 —

Read these verses and note what happens when we are faithful:

Genesis 39:4-6—

Proverbs 28:20—

Matthew 24:45-47—

Matthew 25:14-23—

Prayer in the Life of Samuel

Both prayer and faithfulness made up the inner fiber of this great man's life. From the beginning of Samuel's life of service, God shows us through Samuel that faithfulness in the little things qualifies us to be trusted with greater things.

Samuel was faithful to respond to God's voice—Read these verses from 1 Samuel and note what they tell us about Samuel's birth and early days:

1:1-2—

1:9-11 and 17—

1:19-20—

1:24-28—

2:11 and 18—

Now read 1 Samuel 3:1-10.

To whom did the Lord choose to speak?

How many times did the Lord speak?

What did the priest Eli discern and advise?

How did Samuel finally respond?

What can you learn from Samuel about the right response to God's direction?

Samuel was faithful to God's standards—Read these scriptures from 1 Samuel and note what they tell us about the standards practiced by Samuel's parents and impressed upon Samuel as he was growing up under the tutelage of his parents and Eli, the priest:

1:3—

1:11 (see also Numbers 6:1-5)—

1:22-28—

2:1-10—

2:18—

What was the result of God's grace, the standards set in Samuel's early life, and Samuel's obedience, as seen in 1 Samuel 3:19-21?

How did Samuel exhibit his faithfulness to God's standards in the course of leading God's people, as seen in 1 Samuel 7:1-3?

How can you be more faithful to God's standards

in your own daily life—

as a parent—

as an employee and coworker—

as a citizen—

Samuel was faithful to pray for God's people—For whom and how do you see Samuel praying in 1 Samuel:

7:5-9—

12:19-23—

15:10-11—

As you look at your prayer list for others, how is your faithfulness to pray for God's people revealed?

What changes need to be made?

Samuel was faithful to seek God's help through prayer—Read 1 Samuel 7:7-14.

Describe the problem and solution concerning God's people.

What did the people do about their situation, and what was Samuel's role?

How did God reveal Himself on behalf of His people?

Samuel was faithful to continue to pray for God's people—Read 1 Samuel 8:1-9.

What request did the people make of Samuel (verse 5)?

How did Samuel respond, and what were God's instructions (verses 6-9)?

After Samuel anointed Saul to be king over the Israelites, what promise did Samuel make to the people in 1 Samuel 12:23?

How can you be more faithful in praying for those who have disappointed you?

Samuel was faithful to follow God to the end—Read 1 Samuel 16:1-4.

What command did God give to Samuel, what was his initial reaction, and what did Samuel do anyway?

Prayer Principles for Your Life

Write out the prayer principles from the life of Samuel below (see pages 73-75 in your book):

1.

2.

3.

4.

5.

Which one or two principles encourage you most as you pray for the issues you are presently facing, and why?

What about Samuel's prayer life do you want to remember, and why?

Chapter 5

David...
a Man of Remarkable Trust

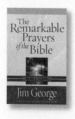 In *The Remarkable Prayers of the Bible*, read again each "Lesson to Learn about Prayer" from the chapter entitled "David...a Man of Remarkable Trust." Which lesson about prayer offered you the greatest motivation or instruction for your prayer life, and why?

Which offered you the greatest challenge to your prayer life, and why?

Trusting the Lord

Look up the verb *trust* in a dictionary and write the definition here:

How does this definition help you to understand your relationship with God?

According to Isaiah 26:4, why is it good to place your trust in God?

Read Proverbs 3:5-6. Where are you instructed to put your trust, and to what extent?

Where are you *not* to put your trust?

How is a firm trust in the Lord evidenced?

What results from putting your trust in God?

Read Jeremiah 17:5-8. In verse 5, what two things does the "cursed" person trust in, and what effect does this have on his relationship with God?

How does verse 6 further describe this person's life without God?

By contrast, whom does the "blessed" person trust (verse 7)?

How does verse 8 describe this "blessed" person's life?

The Bible warns against placing your trust in anything other than God. According to the following scriptures, where do the foolish and wicked place their trust?

Proverbs 11:28 —   Isaiah 42:17 —

Proverbs 28:26 —   Luke 18:9 —

According to these verses, what happens when you put your trust in God?

Psalm 32:10—

Proverbs 16:20—

Proverbs 28:25—

Isaiah 26:3—

In what ways does trusting in God affect your life, according to Psalm 37:3-5?

Prayer in the Life of David

David was a man who delighted in pouring forth his soul to God. In the Bible, he chronicled for us his hopes, fears, triumphs, disappointments, and labors in prayers—uttered all through his life. The lifelong exercise of prayer led David to an understanding of God and a deep, abiding trust in Him.

David trusted God—Read these scriptures from 1 Samuel 17 and note how David's trust in God was evidenced:

Verses 33-35—

Verses 36-37—

Verses 45-47—

What impossible odds are you up against? Rehearse God's faithfulness to you in the past, then pray and trust in Him.

David sought God's direction—Read again (on pages 81-82 in your book) about the times David sought direction from God.

What battles are you headed into, and how can you follow David's example and "inquire of the Lord" through prayer?

David thirsted for God—Read Psalm 63:1-2 and Acts 13:22.

Note the ways David's thirst for God is described and defined.

David understood the value of time—Read David's prayer in Psalm 39:4-5.

How did David describe his life?

What was his prayer request to God?

How would constant awareness of the value of time and the shortness of life change your approach to each day?

David asked for forgiveness—Read 2 Samuel 11:1-27.

In a few sentences, describe the extent of David's sin with Bathsheba.

What did David say about his sin in 2 Samuel 12:13?

Scan through Psalm 32 and 51 and note four or five blessings that accompany true repentance.

Write out the two lessons to learn from David's prayers of confessions (see pages 85-86 in your book). Are there any steps you need to take to restore a right relationship with God?

David had an understanding of God—Read Psalm 139. List the truths about God emphasized in:

Verses 1-6—

Verses 7-12—

Verses 13-18—

Check any truths that are new to your understanding of God.

David prayed from a grateful heart—Read from pages 87-88 in your book about others who, like David, prayed from a grateful heart. Then read 2 Samuel 7:12-16.

List several ways David expressed his gratitude to God through prayer in verses 18-29.

For what are you thankful today? Have you shared your gratitude with God? If not, it's time to do so.

Prayer Principles for Your Life

Write out the prayer principles from the life of David below (see pages 90-92 in your book):

1.

2.

3.

4.

Which one or two principles encourage you most as you pray for the issues you are presently facing, and why?

What about David's prayer life do you want to remember, and why?

$\mathcal{N}$ehemiah...

a Man of Remarkable Purpose

In *The Remarkable Prayers of the Bible*, read again each "Lesson to Learn about Prayer" from the chapter entitled "Nehemiah...a Man of Remarkable Purpose." Which lesson about prayer offered you the greatest motivation or instruction for your prayer life, and why?

Which offered you the greatest challenge to your prayer life, and why?

Purpose Begins with God

What insights do these scriptures give about the importance of setting God as the ultimate priority in your life?

Proverbs 19:21—

Matthew 6:33—

Ephesians 5:8-10—

Philippians 3:12-14—

2 Timothy 2:15—

What advice do these verses give for fulfilling God's purpose for your life?

1 Corinthians 9:24-26—

Hebrews 10:35-36—

Hebrews 12:1-2—

What practices are involved in determining God's purpose, according to these verses?

Psalm 63:6-7—

Proverbs 3:6—

Proverbs 15:22—

Matthew 7:7-8—

What does the Bible say in these scriptures about God's purpose for all believers?

John 17:20-23—

Ephesians 4:1-3 —

Philippians 2:14-15 —

1 Thessalonians 4:3 —

Read Psalm 37:3-5. What are we as Christians called to focus upon? What will result when we do these things?

Read 1 Corinthians 10:31. What should be our goal in our every endeavor?

Prayer in the Life of Nehemiah

Turning to God in prayer is the starting point for compre-hending how what is happening to you fits into God's purpose. Nehemiah instructs you in the fine art of praying when you need to seek God's will and gain an understanding of what He is allowing to take place in your life.

Nehemiah prayed for direction — Read Nehemiah 1:1-11.

Who was Nehemiah (end of verse 11), and what news did he receive in verses 1-3?

Describe Nehemiah's response to the report in verse 4.

Describe the content of Nehemiah's prayer as revealed in:

Verse 5—

Verse 6—

Verse 7—

Verses 8-10—

Verse 11—

What impresses you most about Nehemiah's prayer for God's direction?

Nehemiah prayed on the spot—Read Nehemiah 2:1-8.

What did the king ask Nehemiah, and why (verses 1-2)?

How did Nehemiah reply (verse 3)?

When the king asked for Nehemiah's request, what did Nehemiah do, and for what did he ask (verses 5-8)?

What was the result of Nehemiah's on-the-spot prayer and his dialogue with the king (verse 8)?

Nehemiah prayed for deliverance—Read Nehemiah 4:1-9.

How did Nehemiah "answer" and deal with the outside mockery and conspiracy he encountered as the Jews began building the wall (verses 4-5 and 9)?

Now read Nehemiah 4:10-23. In a few sentences, list several ways Nehemiah encouraged the Israelites.

How did the Israelites go about building the wall in the face of their enemies?

What do you learn about balancing dependence upon God with personal action and vigilance?

Nehemiah prayed for restitution — Read Nehemiah 5:1-13.

Briefly note several of the problems that surfaced among God's people as they sought to rebuild the wall.

How did Nehemiah "call down" the wrath of God on anyone who failed to release the debts of their brethren in verse 13?

Now read Nehemiah 5:14-19. List the highlights regarding Nehemiah's selfless example. How did he end his recorded reflection?

Nehemiah prayed in confession —Read Nehemiah 9:1-38.

What did the people do to themselves as they worshiped God after building the wall of Jerusalem (verses 1-3)?

Note two or three personal impressions from the lengthy prayer of the priests (the Levites) in verses 5-37.

What elements of Nehemiah 9 would you like to incorporate in your worship and prayers?

Nehemiah prayed for remembrance —Read the utterances from Nehemiah's prayers as cited on page 104 of your book. In each instance, what was Nehemiah's request to God, and for what reason?

Verse 14—

Verses 15-22—

Verses 29-31—

For what service to God's people will you be—or would you like to be—remembered? What actions or changes would more quickly move you toward living out God's purposes for you?

Prayer Principles for Your Life

Write out the prayer principles from the life of Nehemiah below (see pages 107-08 in your book):

1.

2.

3.

4.

Which one or two principles encourage you most as you pray for the issues you are presently facing, and why?

What about Nehemiah's prayer life do you want to remember, and why?

Chapter 7

Job...
a Man of Remarkable Character

In *The Remarkable Prayers of the Bible*, read again each "Lesson to Learn about Prayer" from the chapter entitled "Job...a Man of Remarkable Character." Which lesson about prayer offered you the greatest motivation or instruction for your prayer life, and why?

Which offered you the greatest challenge to your prayer life, and why?

Character Forged in Suffering

Write out a definition for the word *character* from your dictionary as used in relation to a person's life:

The world has its standards for a man or woman's character, but what did Jesus say in Matthew 5:48 regarding the standard for your character?

Obviously, you won't achieve Jesus' standard while here on earth, but what does 1 John 3:2-3 say you can look forward to in the future?

What do these verses say about how God develops our character?

Genesis 22:1-12 —

Romans 5:3-4 —

James 1:2-4 —

1 Peter 1:6-7—

Read Job 1:1–2:10. How is Job's character described in Job 1:1 and 8?

What explanation did Satan give for Job's success, according to Job 1:9-10?

In Job 1:11, what did Satan say would happen if God took His hand of protection away from Job?

Compare Job 1:8 and 2:10. How did Job's trials and suffering affect his character?

Prayer in the Life of Job

Just mention the name *Job,* and most people think of pain and suffering. Yet it was this very agony that strengthened Job's character even more.

Job prayed a prayer of intercession—Read Job 1:1-12.

How is Job described in verses 1-5?

What do you learn about Satan from Job 1:6-12?

Now read Job 1:4-5 and 42:10. In both the first and last chapters of the book of Job, what do you see Job doing?

For whom did Job pray in Job 1:4-5, and why?

For whom did Job pray in Job 42:7-10, and what were the results?

In what ways can you increase your prayers for your family and friends?

Job prayed a prayer of resignation — Read Job 1:13-21.

Briefly outline what happened to Job's family (verses 13-19).

When tragedy struck his family, how did Job respond (verses 20-21)?

What was Job's understanding of God as expressed in Job 1:21 and 2:10?

Job prayed a prayer of self-pity — Read Job 2:1-10.

Briefly outline what happened to Job physically.

When physical suffering came Job's way, what did his wife say (verse 9)?

How did Job respond to his wife and to God's dealings in his life (verse 10)?

Job prayed a prayer for understanding — Read Job 10:1-22.

Most of the book of Job (Job 3:1–37:24) contains dialogue between Job and his three friends. As Job wearied under the continued accusations of his friends, how did he respond, according to Job 10:2?

Briefly describe what Job says about his situation and suffering in Job 10.

Now read Luke 1:26-38. What was it that Mary did not understand, and what was her attitude even in the midst of her situation (verse 38)?

Compare Job's prayer and attitude with Mary's better way of praying to God and asking for understanding about the events and suffering in life that don't make sense. Write out your observations.

Job prayed a prayer of supplication — Read Job 23:1-5.

How does Job describe His interaction with God in verses 4 and 5?

Look up the word *supplication* in a dictionary and write a brief definition of the word here.

Evaluate your habit of supplication concerning the issues you face in your daily life. How can you be more steadfast in entreating God for His help and understanding?

Job prayed a prayer of repentance — Read Job 42:1-6.

These utterances follow four chapters (Job 38–41) of God speaking face to face to Job. What did Job proclaim about God's character and abilities?

What did Job admit about himself?

Now read Job 42:10-17, and describe the last days of Job's life.

Prayer Principles for Your Life

Write out the prayer principles from the life of Job below (see pages 121-23 in your book):

1.

2.

3.

4.

Which one or two principles encourage you most as you pray for the issues you are presently facing, and why?

What about Job's prayer life do you want to remember, and why?

Chapter 8

*J*eremiah...
a Man of Remarkable Determination

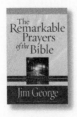

In *The Remarkable Prayers of the Bible*, read again each "Lesson to Learn about Prayer" from the chapter entitled "Jeremiah...a Man of Remarkable Determination." Which lesson about prayer offered you the greatest motivation or instruction for your prayer life, and why?

Which offered you the greatest challenge to your prayer life, and why?

Firmness of Purpose

What should be the focus of your determination, according to:

Joshua 24:14 —

Psalm 1:1-2 —

John 15:4-5 —

What sober warnings do the following scriptures give concerning those who do not have a focused determination to know and serve God?

John 15:6 —

Luke 18:18-25 —

What do these verses from Proverbs 4 say you can do to shape your conduct?

Verse 23 —

Verse 24—

Verse 25—

Verse 26—

Verse 27—

In the following passages, write out the phrase that indicates the spirit of determination in each of these men and women in the Bible:

Moses in Exodus 32:31-32—

Esther in Esther 4:13-16—

David in 2 Samuel 24:21-24—

Jesus in:

Luke 2:49—

Luke 9:51—

Luke 22:42—

Paul in:

Acts 21:10-13—

Philippians 1:21—

Philippians 3:13-14—

What does Paul say should be a balanced determination for all Christians, according to Philippians 1:23-25?

What improvements must you make to strengthen your determination to live out God's purpose?

Prayer in the Life of Jeremiah

Jeremiah lived through hard times brought about by his own people, yet he remained obedient to God and faithful in prayer.

Jeremiah's prayer of inability—Read Jeremiah 1:1-10.

What do you learn about:

Jeremiah's heritage (verses 1-3)—

Jeremiah's "call" from God (verses 4-5)—

Jeremiah's initial response to God's call (verse 6)—

God's assurances to Jeremiah (verses 7-10)—

What are some of the excuses you sometimes give for not obeying God and doing His will? Can you think of any assurances of God's enabling power and assistance to you as stated in the Bible? Note a few of them here.

Jeremiah's prayer of concern—Read Jeremiah 2:1-2.

This begins the first of God's messages to Israel through Jeremiah. As the prediction of Israel's doom continued, how did Jeremiah begin his response in Jeremiah 4:10?

How did Jeremiah express concern for the people in verse 19?

Take a look at your prayer list. Is a concern for others reflected on your list? What are some concerns you can express to God on behalf of others?

Jeremiah was told not to pray—Read these scriptures and note in each instance what God told Jeremiah, and why:

Jeremiah 7:16—

Jeremiah 11:14—

Jeremiah 14:11-12—

God's people needed to change their lifestyle. What in your life needs immediate attention, and what will you do about it?

Jeremiah prayed for direction—Read Jeremiah 10:17-24.

In a few words, what was God's message to the people in verses 17-18?

In a few words, how did God express His grief in verse 19?

Why was God grieved, according to verses 20-22?

Describe Jeremiah's prayer for direction and correction in verses 23-24.

What instructions do the following scriptures give you regarding seeking God's direction?

　　　Jeremiah 10:23—

　　　Psalm 139:23-24—

　　　Proverbs 3:6—

Jeremiah prayed for justice — Read Jeremiah 11:18–12:2.

What details do you learn in Jeremiah 11:18-19 about the plot to kill Jeremiah?

How did Jeremiah pray about this demise in Jeremiah 11:20, and how did God reply in verses 21-23?

In Jeremiah 12:1-2, Jeremiah once again prayed. What was the general question he posed to God?

Jeremiah prayed for relief — Read Jeremiah 12:3-6.

Once Jeremiah finished asking God about the wicked, in what direction did he turn his prayers (verse 3)?

What did Jeremiah say to God in:

        Verse 3 —

        Verse 4 —

What reality check did God give Jeremiah in verses 5-6?

How can you nurture or improve the habit of turning to God through prayer in the midst of life's perplexing moments?

Jeremiah prayed in doubt—Read Jeremiah 32:16-27.

After Jeremiah obeyed God's instructions to purchase a field, he began to have doubts. What did He pray to God (verses 16-25), and how did God answer (verses 26-27)?

How did God encourage Jeremiah in Jeremiah 33:1-3?

How does God's word to His prophet Jeremiah in 32:27 and 33:3 encourage you to pray?

Prayer Principles for Your Life

Write out the prayer principles from the life of Jeremiah below (see pages 137-40 in your book):

1.

2.

3.

4.

5.

6.

Which one or two principles encourage you most as you pray for the issues you are presently facing, and why?

What about Jeremiah's prayer life do you want to remember, and why?

Chapter 9

$\mathcal{D}$aniel...
a Man of Remarkable Integrity

In *The Remarkable Prayers of the Bible*, read again each "Lesson to Learn about Prayer" from the chapter entitled "Daniel...a Man of Remarkable Integrity." Which lesson about prayer offered you the greatest motivation or instruction for your prayer life, and why?

Which offered you the greatest challenge to your prayer life, and why?

Living a Life of Integrity

List the seven things God says He hates, according to Proverbs 6:16-19:

—   —

—   —

—   —

—

Integrity involves what you say and what you do. How does Hannah show us this aspect of integrity in 1 Samuel 1?

Her vow in verse 11 (see also verses 19-20) —

Her fulfillment of her vow in verses 24-28 —

Integrity indicates faithfulness. What are Jesus' comments on faithfulness in Luke 16:

Verse 10—

Verse 11—

Verse 12—

Integrity also involves being dependable. Read Acts 13:1-13.

Who were the members of this first missionary team (verses 1-5)?

What were John's duties (verse 5)?

Briefly describe what happened when the team arrived on the island of Cyprus (verses 6-12).

What resulted when the team left the island (verse 13)?

Godly men and women are described by various words in the Bible. Read these verses and note the names or facts about the people and any words used to describe their integrity:

Judges 6:11-12 —

Proverbs 31:10-12

Acts 13:22 —

Philippians 2:14-15 —

1 Timothy 3:2 —

1 Timothy 3:10 —

1 Timothy 3:11—

Prayer in the Life of Daniel

Prayer was a vital part of Daniel's secret to a life of holiness and integrity. His prayer life helped develop him into a man who was blameless. As a prophet and a statesman, Daniel served God and His causes for more than 80 years.

Daniel was habitual in prayer—Read these scriptures and make notes regarding Daniel's habit of prayer:

Daniel 2:16-18—

Daniel 6:10-11—

Daniel 9:1-4—

Daniel 10:1-3,12—

Daniel 12:8—

What one thing will you do today to strengthen your personal habit of prayer?

Daniel prayed in an emergency—Read Daniel 2:1-18.

In a few sentences, describe the scene and Daniel's response.

Now read these verses and describe the results:

Verses 19-30—

Verses 46-49—

How do you think the regular habit of prayer equips and prepares you for praying in an emergency?

Daniel was a man of exacting prayer—Read Daniel 2:14-23 again.

For what did Daniel specifically ask his three friends to pray (verse 18)?

Again, how did God answer this specific prayer request, according to verses 46-49?

How did Daniel acknowledge and praise God for His attributes in verses 20-23?

How would praying more specifically about your concerns improve your prayer requests?

Daniel prayed for his people — Read Daniel 9:1-19.

What prompted Daniel's prayer session (verses 1-2)?

How did Daniel prepare for this time of prayer (verse 3)?

How did Daniel approach and address God (verse 4)?

Briefly note how Daniel spoke to God regarding the sins of the people, including himself (verses 5-15).

Briefly note the requests in Daniel's appeal to God on behalf of his people (verses 16-19).

Daniel prayed with the right attitude — Review Daniel 9:3-5.

In a few words describe:

Daniel's attitude toward the act of prayer (verse 3) —

Daniel's attitude toward God (verse 4) —

Daniel's attitude toward sin (verse 5) —

Now read Daniel 9:20-23. How do you see God answering Daniel's prayer?

How do you normally approach God on behalf of others, and what aspects of Daniel's pattern do you want to incorporate in the future?

Daniel maintained the honor of the true God—Read again (on page 152 in your book) about Daniel's effect and influence on others for the causes of God. What did these pagan leaders admit and confess regarding God?

Nebuchadnezzar in Daniel 2:47—

Nebuchadnezzar in Daniel 4:2-3—

Darius in Daniel 6:26—

How do you see Daniel being salt in a pagan society and living out Jesus' later command to believers to "let your light so shine before men, that they may see your good works and glorify your Father in heaven" (Matthew 5:16)?

Can you think of ways your prayers and conduct have influenced others toward God? Can you think of any changes you must make in your own life?

Prayer Principles for Your Life

Write out the prayer principles from the life of Daniel below (see pages 154-56 in your book):

1.

2.

3.

4.

5.

Which one or two principles encourage you most as you pray for the issues you are presently facing, and why?

What about Daniel's prayer life do you want to remember, and why?

Chapter 10
*M*ary...
a Woman of Remarkable Worship

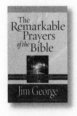 In *The Remarkable Prayers of the Bible*, read again each "Lesson to Learn about Prayer" from the chapter entitled "Mary...a Woman of Remarkable Worship." Which lesson about prayer offered you the greatest motivation or instruction for your prayer life, and why?

Which offered you the greatest challenge to your prayer life, and why?

The Nature of Worship

Who is it we are to worship as revealed in these verses, and why?

Exodus 34:14—

Psalm 95:6—

Luke 4:8—

What attitudes and conditions are involved in true worship, according to:

1 Samuel 15:22—

Psalm 24:3-4—

Hosea 6:6—

Micah 6:6-8—

John 4:24—

Hebrews 13:15—

James 4:8-10—

Read Acts 2:42-47. What are some of the elements that were involved in worship in the early church (verses 42 and 47)?

How often did this worship take place (verse 42 and 46)?

Where did this worship take place (verse 46)?

List some of the feelings and experiences that resulted from the nature of the worship shared by the members of the new church in Jerusalem (Acts 2:43-47).

What is the value of true worship, as shown in these passages?

Psalm 50:23 —

Acts 2:42-47 —

Read John 4:19-24. Where did some of the people of Jesus' day believe they had to go in order to worship (verse 20)?

What did Jesus say was more important than the place of worship (verse 23)?

How does Jesus define true worshipers, and why (verses 23-24)?

Read Revelation 15:2-4. What will the true followers of the Lord do in heaven (verse 3)?

Prayer in the Life of Mary

From her encounter with the angel Gabriel as a teen to her attendance at the prayer meeting held in the upper room as a widow and after the death of her Son, Mary is seen in the Bible as a woman who worshiped and prayed.

Mary exhibited a spirit of humility—Read Luke 1:46-55.

Then read again (on pages 161-62 in your book) about Mary's humility as prayed in her "Magnificat." Make your own notes concerning:

Verse 47—

Verse 48—

Verse 49—

Now read again (on pages 162-63 in your book) about the examples of others in the Bible who expressed humility. Of the instances and utterances in these examples, which one instructs you most regarding humility, and why?

Mary gave the right response to revelation — Read Luke 1:26-38.

List the ways Mary demonstrated a humble spirit.

How does Mary's response to God's revelation concerning His will for her life convict or instruct you regarding your acceptance and response to God's plan for you?

Mary worshiped with others — Read Luke 1:39-55.

Who was present at this time of worship?

Briefly describe the interchange and worship that occurred. What components of worship do you see in this encounter?

Now quickly read through Acts 1:1-14.

Briefly describe the events that led up to verses 12-14.

What occurred in verses 12-14, and who was present?

What does this reveal about Mary:

As a pray-er—

As a worshiper—

Who are the others you pray with? If this vital part of your Christian experience, prayer life, and worship is lacking, what will you do to integrate it into your worship?

Mary's heart was saturated with God's Word—Read again Luke 1:46-55. At least a dozen references to Old Testament scriptures are contained in Mary's outpouring of praise and worship.

Now read again Hannah's prayer in 1 Samuel 2:1-10 and note any similarities you observe in Mary's and Hannah's prayers.

Luke 1	**1 Samuel 2**
46-47	1
49	2
51	4,9-10
52	8
53	5,7

Both Mary and Hannah worshiped God through prayer out of hearts and souls saturated with the Word of God. What must you do to:

Saturate your heart with Scripture—

Add more Scripture verses and truths to your prayers—

Mary had faith in God—Read again Luke 1:26-38. List the ways Mary demonstrated faith and confidence in God.

How does Mary's faith and trust in God instruct or convict you?

Prayer Principles for Your Life

Write out the prayer principles from the life of Mary below (see pages 170-72 in your book):

1.

2.

3.

4.

5.

Which one or two principles encourage you most as you pray for the issues you are presently facing, and why?

What about Mary's prayer life do you want to remember, and why?

Chapter 11

$\mathcal{P}$aul...
a Man of Remarkable Passion

In *The Remarkable Prayers of the Bible*, read again each "Lesson to Learn about Prayer" from the chapter entitled "Paul...a Man of Remarkable Passion." Which lesson about prayer offered you the greatest motivation or instruction for your prayer life, and why?

Which offered you the greatest challenge to your prayer life, and why?

Living with Passion and Purpose

Passion is often defined as strong feeling, enthusiasm, and motivation. The Bible often uses the word *zeal* to describe one who is passionate about something or someone.

What do these verses teach about Christ and His example of passion and zeal?

John 2:17 (see also Psalm 69:9) —

Hebrews 12:2-3 —

Look again at Hebrews 12:2-3. What does Christ's example in verse 3 teach you about the way you deal with criticism and persecution?

Unfortunately, passion and zeal can at times work contrary to God's ways. How was zeal misdirected in these instances?

Paul's life before Christ in Galatians 1:13-14 —

The Jews in Romans 10:2 —

Read 1 Corinthians 10:31. What do you learn here about the right purpose and motivation for your zeal in all areas of life?

Read 1 Thessalonians 5:12-13, which describes the zeal that should mark those in church leadership. How are you to respond to such leaders?

Read Romans 12:11-13. List the purposes and actions you are to be passionate about as a Christian.

Read Colossians 3:23-24. What kind of work ethic should you have, and why?

Read 2 Corinthians 9:2. What effect did the zealous giving toward the needs of the poor in Jerusalem have upon others?

Read 2 Timothy 1:6-7. What was Paul's exhortation to his young disciple, Timothy, when Timothy lost some of his zeal?

What was the source of this passion (verse 7)?

Read 2 Corinthians 11:23-29, where Paul lists what he was able to endure due to God's grace and his own zeal for the things of Christ. How do you rate your present zeal for serving the Lord, and what steps must you take to fan the flames of your passion?

How do you think prayer helps?

Prayer in the Life of Paul

Paul is one of the most significant figures the Christian faith has ever produced. In the Bible we learn that the focus and force of Paul's life and ministry was prayer.

Paul prayed for direction — Read Acts 13:1-2.

What direction did the church in Antioch receive here, and how was it obtained?

Paul prayed and fasted — Read the scriptures below and note the outcome of prayer and fasting:

Acts 13:1-3 —

Acts 14:21-23 —

Paul's prayers were strategic —Read Colossians 1:1-12 and note:

For whom Paul prayed (verse 2) —

How Paul prayed (verses 3 and 9) —

Now read, on pages 178-79 in your book, through the specifics of Paul's prayers for the Colossian believers. How can you use Paul's prayer as a guide for praying:

For yourself —

For those in your family —

For your friends —

For those in your church—

For believers around the world—

Paul's prayers were continuous—Read (on pages 180-81 in your book) about Paul's continual attitude of prayer.

What does it mean to "pray always" and "without ceasing"?

Why would developing such a habit be beneficial?

Paul's prayers were for other people—Read the verses that follow and note Paul's references to prayer for others:

Romans 1:9-10—

1 Corinthians 1:4—

Philippians 1:3-6—

Colossians 1:3-4—

1 Thessalonians 1:2-4—

2 Thessalonians 1:11-12—

2 Timothy 1:3-4—

Philemon 4-6—

Following Paul's example, how can you better pray for others?

Paul asked for prayer from others—Read the following prayer requests from Paul, noting his specific request in each:

Romans 15:30-31—

2 Corinthians 1:11—

Ephesians 6:18—

Colossians 4:3—

For which of these solicitations do you also need help? Make a list of faithful pray-ers, and ask them for their prayer support.

Paul's prayers were in faith—Read the scriptures that follow and note what they say about prayer:

Matthew 21:22—

1 John 5:14-15—

What do the above passages tell you about how you can pray with more confidence?

Prayer Principles for Your Life

Write out the prayer principles from the life of Paul below (see pages 187-88 in your book):

1.

2.

3.

4.

Which one or two principles encourage you most as you pray for the issues you are presently facing, and why?

What about Paul's prayer life do you want to remember, and why?

Chapter 12

*J*esus...
a Man of Remarkable Prayer

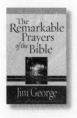

In *The Remarkable Prayers of the Bible*, read again each "Lesson to Learn about Prayer" from the chapter entitled "Jesus...a Man of Remarkable Prayer." Which lesson about prayer offered you the greatest motivation or instruction for your prayer life, and why?

Which offered you the greatest challenge to your prayer life, and why?

The Perfect Model in Prayer

Jesus lived in the spirit of prayer. Prayer was His life, His habit. Looking at the life and prayers of Jesus provides us with the perfect model for prayer.

Jesus prayed before important events or decisions—Read these verses in your Bible and describe each event or decision in your own words:

The beginning of His ministry (Luke 3:21-22)—

The choosing of His leaders (Luke 6:12-16)—

The need to encourage and strengthen (Matthew 16:21–17:1 and Luke 9:28-29)—

The completion of His ministry (Matthew 26:36-46)—

How does Jesus' example prepare you to better handle your next major event or decision?

Jesus was in the habit of praying — Read these verses in your Bible and briefly describe the circumstances surrounding Jesus' times of prayer:

Mark 1:32-37 —

Luke 5:15-16—

Luke 10:1-2 and 17-21—

John 11:39-44—

Luke 22:31-32—

Luke 6:27-28 and 23:34—

Luke 23:46—

What will it take for you to develop a more consistent habit of prayer? Write out two or three steps you will take.

Jesus taught about prayer with fasting — Read the verses below and comment on what they teach you about fasting and the importance Jesus placed on fasting:

Matthew 6:16-18 —

Matthew 17:14-21 —

Luke 4:2-13 —

Luke 5:33-35 —

Share an experience when you fasted and prayed. What was the reason, what did you do, and what were the results?

How can you make fasting a regular part of your prayer life?

Jesus taught others how to pray—Read both Matthew 6:9-13 and Luke 11:1-4. Then read through the outline of "The Lord's Prayer" on page 198 in your book.

Which elements of Jesus' pattern for prayer are missing from your prayers?

Take five minutes and pray, following Jesus' model prayer and incorporating each of the elements into your prayer.

Jesus prayed for others—Read John 17:1-26 and write out in your own words for whom Jesus prayed and what He requested of the Father on their behalf:

John 17:1-6—

John 17:6-19—

John 17:20-26—

Jesus prayed for prayer assistance—Read the verses that follow, and note the assistance Jesus promised you as you go through life and its trials:

John 14:16-17—

Romans 8:26-27—

Hebrews 7:25—

How do these truths and promises comfort you in your difficulties and encourage you as you pray?

Prayer Principles for Your Life

Write out the prayer principles from the life of Jesus below (see pages 202-03 in your book):

1.

2.

3.

4.

Which one or two principles encourage you most as you pray for the issues you are presently facing, and why?

What about Jesus' prayer life do you want to remember, and why?

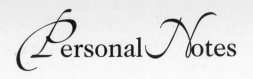

Personal Notes

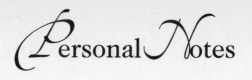

Personal Notes

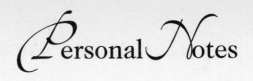

Personal Notes

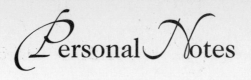

Personal Notes

Other Books by Jim George

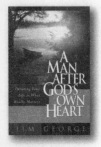

A Man After God's Own Heart

Many Christian men want to be men after God's own heart...but how do they do this? George shows that a heartfelt desire to practice God's priorities is all that's needed. God's grace does the rest.

A Husband After God's Own Heart

Husbands will find their marriages growing richer and deeper as they pursue God and discover 12 areas in which they can make a real difference in their relationship with their wife.

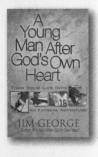

A Young Man After God's Own Heart

Pursuing God really *is* an adventure—a lot like climbing a mountain. There are all kinds of challenges on the way up, but the awesome view at the top is well worth the trip. This book helps young men to experience the thrill of knowing real success in life—the kind that counts with God.

God's Man of Influence

How can a man have a lasting impact? Here are the secrets to having a positive and meaningful influence in the lives of everyone a man meets. This book will help men define the goals that give their lives direction and purpose.

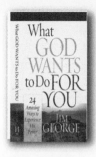

What God Wants to Do for You
(coauthored with Elizabeth George)
Explore 24 special promises from the Bible that
will draw you closer to God. Each chapter con-
cludes with instant practical applications on
how to benefit immediately from each promise.
Available March 2006

God Loves His Precious Children
(coauthored with Elizabeth George)
Jim and Elizabeth George share the
comfort and assurance of Psalm 23 with
young children. Engaging watercolor
scenes and delightful rhymes bring the
truths of each verse to life.

God's Wisdom for Little Boys
(coauthored with Elizabeth George)
The wonderful teachings of Proverbs
come to life for boys. Memorable rhymes
play alongside colorful paintings for an
exciting presentation of truths to live
by.

An Invitation to Write

Jim George is a teacher and speaker and the author of several books, including *A Man After God's Own Heart*. If you would like to receive more information about other books and audio products by Jim George, to sign up for his mailings, or to share how *The Remarkable Prayers of the Bible* has influenced your life, you can write to Jim at:

Jim George
P.O. Box 2879
Belfair, WA 98528
Toll-free fax/phone: 1-800-542-4611
www.JimGeorge.com